PRIVATIZATION NOW OR ELSE

The Impending Failure of Democracy and Freedom in Central Europe

Thomas Gale Moore

1991

Hoover Institution
Stanford University

Essays in Public Policy No. 21

First printing, 1991

Manufactured in the United States of America
95 94 93 92 91 9 8 7 6 5 4 3 2 1

Library of Congress Cataloging in Publication Data

Moore, Thomas Gale
Privatization now or else: the impending failure of democracy and freedom in central europe / Thomas Gale Moore.

p. cm. — (Essays in public policy; no. 21)
Includes bibliographical references.
ISBN 0-8179-5262-4
1. Privatization—Central Europe. 2. Central Europe—Economic Policy. 3. Economic Stabilization—Central Europe.
I. Title. II. Series.
HC244.M574 1991
338.947—dc20 91-8781
CIP

Contents

Introduction

By 1992, the Common Market may have removed all barriers to the internal flow of people and goods, while raising a new Berlin Wall between it and the former East bloc countries. Stagnation, deteriorating economies, and a lack of opportunities in Poland, Czechoslovakia, Hungary, Romania, Bulgaria, and Yugoslavia are likely to produce the most massive illegal immigration the world has ever seen, an exodus of crisis proportions. Only a successful reform of these economies can stave off this tragedy.

The former Communist countries of Central Europe are facing hard times. After January 1, 1991, oil, which the Soviet Union had sold for rubles at prices nominally below world prices, must be paid for in dollars. The Iraq-Kuwait crisis has pushed oil prices to levels not seen since 1980. In addition, the collapse of the Council for Mutual Economic Assistance (CMEA) trading system and the integration of East Germany into West Germany have played havoc with the former East bloc countries' foreign trade.

All this comes on top of economies saddled with bloated, inefficient enterprises. These government-owned units are overstaffed and grossly inefficient, use obsolete technology, and produce poor-quality goods that cannot be sold in the world market. Many should be closed down, and others need restructuring; all need to be converted to private ownership.

Officials in Czechoslovakia, Hungary, and Poland understand the importance of privatization and recognize that moving to a market-based economy requires reducing the proportion of their economies owned and controlled by the state. Unless governments transfer ownership of their enterprises to private hands, even good macroeconomic policies will fail to prevent the economy from continuing to deteriorate. Investment will be inefficient, and workers will be underemployed; productivity will stagnate or decline. Although encouraging the formation of private firms by citizens and foreigners will diminish the state sector over time, it will be many years before the infirmities of the economy can be significantly improved. Moreover, if the process is allowed to drag on, state enterprises will pressure the government to provide protection from new firms. Experience around the world suggests that too often such protection will be granted, resulting in continued stagnation and inflation.

Private ownership of the means of production is necessary to produce the appropriate incentives for good economic performance. The managers of government-owned firms attempt to please their political superiors; if firms are worker-run, the managers try to please the workers' organizations. Neither type of firm will necessarily seek to minimize costs or maximize profits by catering to their consumers. Worker-managed firms tend to favor the worker over investment or sales; if the firm has access to government funds, wages and salaries will be inflated.

Government-appointed managers often employ superfluous workers who are expected to support those officials overseeing the firm. Sometimes the incentives will favor groups that have strong political influence. Rarely is a government firm motivated to satisfy consumers.

Private enterprises must face the discipline of the market by providing as good or better products than their competitors, satisfying their consumers, and keeping costs below revenues. Thus private managers must maximize profits to avoid being driven out of business or removed from management, making private competitive firms the only guarantee of efficient companies that can make a country productive.

Only an economy with efficient private firms can generate income that improves the standard of living. Comparisons of nonmarket or highly regulated economies with free markets demonstrate the overwhelming superiority of free markets. For example, when the wall fell, the per capita income of East Germany was about half that of West Germany even though both economies started at the same level in 1945. Moreover, because of shorter vacations and longer work weeks, coupled with higher labor force participation rates, real East German living standards were considerably less than half those of its Western compatriots.[1] In addition, East Germany was an ecological disaster.

The problems facing countries attempting to make the transition from a Communist society, where the state owns 80 to 100 percent of all assets, to a private market economy are unprecedented. Never in history has any country made this transformation. Previous privatizations have been small by comparison and implemented in the context of economies that were basically private.

Great Britain privatized less than 10 percent (at most) of its economy over about ten years. Other countries have had even less success. Moreover, Western countries have the benefit of private markets, stock exchanges, meaningful accounting records, labor markets, and a substantial number of individuals with extensive assets who could purchase a significant number of shares in new companies. None of these conditions exists in countries attempting to throw off Marxism.

Western countries can do little to aid or to foster privatization. To the extent it could be used to reduce the heavy debt burden of Poland and Hungary, foreign aid could be useful, but further loans, unless made for purely commercial projects preferably by private lenders, are likely to be wasted and may even slow the transition to a market system by reducing the pressure for change. Probably the single most useful policy the West could follow to aid these former East bloc countries would be to lower or eliminate trade barriers, especially on agriculture. Trade, not aid, is the best medicine.

These countries face the formidable, almost impossible task of privatizing their economies in a short period, but if they fail the alternatives are dismal. In all probability they involve following Latin American patterns of declining standards of living, periods of dictatorship, and, given the proximity of Western Europe, emigration and depletion of the young and vigorous elements of the population. The growing tide of refugees from Central Europe and the Soviet Union indicates that the process is already under way.

SIMILAR PROBLEMS

Although each of the three major Central European countries is different, all face similar difficulties in making the transition. One important difficulty is that property rights are not well defined in any of these countries. Although the state nominally owns all productive assets, no one has clear property rights. Typically, the workers and the managers of enterprises have treated the firms as their own property.

In Poland and Hungary over the last decades, the Communist party has delegated management functions to enterprise or worker councils, which act as if they owned the properties. These councils, which are elected by the employees, choose the manager or at least approve and can fire the manager. Because workers can neither sell the assets nor retain any claim to them once they depart the firm, these councils prefer wage increases to investments. Consequently, firms become decapitalized, letting their equipment and plants deteriorate, and hence become outmoded. Officially the state still owns the assets, but it has little to say about the allocation of resources. Even in Czechoslovakia, which never experimented with worker management, employees act, with the same disastrous results, as if they owned the assets.

Even if the state is the official owner, there may be uncertainty about which governmental body controls the assets: various ministries may claim ownership. To convert an enterprise to private ownership, a national privatization agency may have to dispute property rights with a government ministry. Local or regional government agencies may also claim ownership, meaning that investors do not know who to deal with. In Czechoslovakia, for example, both the Czech and the Slovak governments dispute mineral rights with the national government.

In all these countries, the government is under significant pressure to return property to the previous owners. *Reprivatization*, as it is dubbed, has a strong constituency. After forty years, however, sorting out ownership claims can take considerable time. There have been changes: in some cases properties have been improved at state expense; in others they have been allowed to deteriorate. After a long period of time there may be several claimants to a particular property.

East Germany has shown that attempts to return property to the original owners can hinder investment. Reprivatization raises uncertainty about whether a previous owner will make a claim after the property has been invested in and improved. Property claims by various government bodies are already hindering investments and businesses in the Soviet Union.

Another major issue is the mechanism for privatization. Each country has divided privatization into small privatization, the privatization of small, mainly retail businesses but including services and small manufacturing, and large privatization, the denationalization of larger enterprises, principally those that will become joint stock companies. These countries envision small privatization as an auction of such businesses to the highest bidders.

For chain stores, the plan is to sell each unit separately; however, employees of these concerns have asserted their claim to the properties and demand that they be given priority in purchasing the assets. At the same time, nonemployees argue that these workers should not have any special rights (retail clerks are widely resented for having been discourteous to patrons and able to take advantage of their positions for personal profit; store personnel also often put aside scarce goods for their own use or to sell on the black market).

Both employees and others fear that the sale of small firms to the highest bidder means that former Communist officials, the *nomenklatura*, or black marketers will be the only ones to acquire them, for few others have been in a position to save and build up any capital. Thus there is considerable dissatisfaction with the idea of selling these small enterprises to those making the highest bid, but no one has a better alternative. Consequently, small privatization is being reluctantly supported by the public and the government.

Complicating small privatizations are previous owners who may lay claim to a significant number of small businesses. In Czechoslovakia these could be more than half the total. Given the issues of property rights and employee opposition, privatizing a large percentage of small concerns in the short period that most governments intend may prove impossible.

If the service or retail establishment's building remains in government hands after a firm is privatized, property rights may be poorly defined. For example, in Poland local governments auctioned stores to the highest bidder and then took back the property when another, better offer developed.

Large privatization presents even more difficulties. None of these countries has a working capital market. Hungary has a new stock exchange, but it is small and has little liquidity. Poland plans to establish an exchange in June 1991 in the former headquarters of the Communist party. Stock exchanges, however, cannot touch the underlying problem: the public does not have the assets to purchase large firms. The government could sell at least the profitable firms to foreign investors, but this gives rise to feelings that the "family jewels" are being extorted by foreigners, especially Germans.

Without a market to set a price on those assets, a major issue in selling enterprises is valuation. Most government firms are overstaffed and depend on obsolete technology. What they are worth depends on future earnings, an uncertain sum under the best of circumstances. A proper valuation is important because almost any sale results in charges that the government disposed of the company too cheaply, leading cautious bureaucrats to overprice assets. As a consequence sales are likely to be slow.

These countries have thus decided to hire Western accounting firms, such as Price Waterhouse, Arthur Andersen, and Baker & Mckenzey, to do the evaluations, but these countries' bureaucrats apparently do not realize the uncertainty involved in any valuation, even that of a private firm in a market economy. Attempting to value these enterprises is impossible because the proper data—figures on costs of inputs, capital expenditures, and sales—and the concepts of cost and profit inherent in market-based companies are lacking. Yet all three countries (Czechoslovakia, Hungary, and Poland) plan to have their companies appraised, and although they realize that such estimates will take time, they are all discussing the possibility of having "quick and dirty" valuations performed!

Poland and Czechoslovakia understand that their citizens do not have enough capital to buy those large establishments. Both countries have proposed a voucher scheme that would distribute ownership to their citizens, but neither has fully developed its voucher proposals or plans to rely fully on the voucher. Government ministers have proposed a variety of privatization methods, such as selling stock to locals and foreigners, selling the company in a joint venture, and offering employee stock option plans.

Although authorities in these countries assert the importance of moving fast in privatizing assets, the above-mentioned methods are likely to take years. Some of the more sober time schedules calculate ten years to privatize about 50 to 70 percent of the economy. Unfortunately, that schedule is probably too slow to invigorate an economy that can compete on the world markets and produce significantly higher incomes for the population.

Moreover, this ambitious program may be stalled or slowed by employee opposition. Because the typical firm employs excess labor, workers justifiably fear the prospect of wholesale layoffs (two-thirds is an oft-mentioned figure). If the firm is unprofitable, a private employer may shut it down completely; if it is profitable, the employees will want to acquire the assets.

In both Poland and Hungary, the workers are in a strong position to prevent privatization. In the 1970s and 1980s, most firms in these countries were converted into enterprise councils, with workers electing a large number of the directors. As a result, the employees have been making the major decisions and, as a consequence, believe that they own the firms. Control by these enterprise councils means that the government must renationalize the enterprise to convert it into a joint stock company capable of being privatized. The law in both countries, however, makes it difficult to convert to a joint stock company if the workers oppose the transformation.

DIFFERENCES AMONG THE THREE COUNTRIES

Despite the similarities outlined above, each country remains significantly different from the others, notably in its progress toward privatization. As a metaphor for the differences, consider bananas. In Budapest they were sold in most fruit stores; in Warsaw, where they were being sold by private street vendors but not in state stores, people were walking down the street eating the new treat of bananas. In Prague bananas were unavailable. Those differences reflect the progress each has made toward a market system. Hungary, which has made the most progress in moving toward a market economy, has also privatized more of its industry, albeit only a handful of firms. Poland, which in a relatively short period has moved rapidly to open up its economy, now officially encourages private activity, although only a handful of companies have been privatized. Czechoslovakia has talked about moving to a market system but has made no progress.

Although all three countries project an ambitious program of privatization, only Hungary and Poland have begun to privatize large firms. Most privatizations to date have been spontaneous, which has led to charges that managers have benefited excessively and that the enterprises have been sold too cheaply. There have been several cases where managers have been given lucrative, long-term employment contracts by foreign buyers.

Even in Hungary the first privatization (twenty enterprises) was announced only in September 1990. The State Property Agency, which is in charge of privatization, expects that it will take at least six months to privatize these businesses. The government plans to begin by issuing tenders for accounting firms to value the companies. These Western corporations, after winning contracts to perform the appraisal, must value these concerns in the absence of any meaningful data.

The government will then offer the firms for sale. Prospective buyers are expected to be mainly foreign corporations, although it is hoped that local capital may also be forthcoming. In all countries, despite a lack of alternatives and the fact that Western investors can provide management expertise, a large contingent of the public strongly opposes selling to alien investors.

In Poland the first privatization (seven enterprises) was also announced in September, with the firms to have been in private hands before the end of the year. Although the government failed to meet that deadline, by early January 1991 the stock of five of the concerns had been sold in small lots to individual Polish investors.[2] Czechoslovakia has announced no major privatizations yet or even enacted legislation (as of February 1991) authorizing a change in ownership.

HUNGARY

The Hungarian economy is saddled with a large foreign debt—about $1,500 (U.S. 1988 dollars) for each individual[3] when gross domestic product per capita is about $8,200.[4] (Other estimates of per capita income are as low as $2,300.)[5] Its recent reforms, however, produced a current account surplus in 1990, although the rise in oil prices and the collapse of CMEA are likely to lead to deficits in 1991. Inflation has been running at about 30 percent.[6] Changes in the exchange rate have reduced the black market markup to 10 to 20 percent over the official rate. The state intends to privatize more than 2,500 state-owned enterprises or cooperatives. Enterprise councils control about 75 percent of the businesses, with state ministries controlling the remainder. The government has already privatized the largest travel agency in Hungary and the Tungsram light bulb factory. A wealthy Hungarian purchased a steel mill and improved its performance enough that it earned a profit within one year.

The Hungarian Democratic Forum (HDF), which won the election in June 1990, ran on a platform of privatizing only 40 percent of the state assets in a ten-year period. Since taking office, its position has been that it aims to privatize 70 percent of the assets in three to five years. Many members of the HDF, however, are reluctant to move that fast, and there appears little prospect that such a speedy privatization is feasible even if the will were there. Many people believe that "goulash communism" was at least secure, and they fear unemployment and inflation.

The plans in Hungary are to start privatizing about twenty firms every two months. To do this, the government must identify and structure ten companies a month, a quick pace for the small State Property Agency. Even with this schedule it will take ten years to privatize 1,200 establishments, or about half of all government-owned concerns. The government, however, has stated as its aim privatizing this number in five years, a doubling of its current projected rate.

The State Property Agency (SPA) claims to have privatized some 130 enterprises in 1990, although many of these were the result of spontaneous privatization that occurred before the SPA was formed. At the start of 1991, it asserted that another sixty sales were pending.[7]

According to the government, the actual privatization will take one of three approaches. First, the SPA will identify businesses and parts of large enterprises to be privatized as separate units. If the concern is worker-managed, the SPA will transform the operation into a joint stock corporation. (It is unclear whether the SPA has the authority to do this if the workers' council objects or if the ministry under which the company operates is opposed.) Once the firm has been structured as a joint stock corporation, the SPA will hold all the shares. The SPA can hold onto the enterprise for three years while waiting for the appropriate buyers. The SPA's motivations may be questionable, as in the case of a proposed purchase of a major newspaper by a Swedish newspaper. The SPA stopped the sale, ostensibly on the grounds that a French company would pay more, but the objection was more likely that the French newspaper's political orientation was closer to the HDF (the dominant party in the government) than to that of the Swedish paper.

Second, the concern itself can propose privatization, usually in conjunction with a foreign joint venture. The SPA must determine within thirty days whether to approve the deal, that is, whether the price is right. Although this sounds draconian, the SPA can ask for more information, which starts the thirty-day clock running over again.

Third, any natural person (as differentiated from a corporation) who wants to buy a Hungarian company, including a foreigner, can notify the SPA and the firm of that desire. If the SPA approves the price as fair, the sale will take place. Indeed, on October 18, 1990, the government announced that all Hungarian establishments were up for sale to any person,[8] and the SPA issued a guide for investors on how to buy a government company in a hundred days. Registering with the SPA should trigger an auction, which the agency asserts it will respond to within thirty days, specifying the proportion of foreign ownership permitted and any other conditions. Investors will have ninety days to make their final bids.

Legislation to privatize small firms (small privatization) was passed in July 1990. The government does not plan to privatize banks, but the SPA intends to value stores and auction them to the highest bidder, thus privatizing nine to ten thousand shops. In 1991, the SPA plans to sell 254 shops and service outlets with a minimum bid price of $70,000 a square yard.[9] Stores with more than fifteen employees are not now scheduled for privatization. To promote a Hungarian merchant class, foreigners are prohibited from buying small retail or service organizations.

Although the government has asserted that privatization will be fast, the proposed procedure is likely to be time-consuming. Unless the government is willing to sell cheaply to foreign corporations, it will take time to find buyers, especially Hungarian ones, and to agree on a fair price. Even Lajos Csepi, the current director of the SPA, does not believe that the government's schedule is possible and argues that flooding the market with privatization offerings would rob the country of cash.[10]

Since the SPA's establishment on March 1, 1990, the agency has gone through three heads. It is a controversial post, for if the agency succeeds in selling an enterprise, the charge will almost certainly be made that the price was too low; if it sets high prices, few if any sales will be made. Many in the bureaucracy are opposed to privatization, especially if it means sales to foreign interests, but Hungarians do not have the resources to purchase major firms. Almost all of those with assets are former Communist officials who enriched themselves or black marketeers.

The weight of opinion in Budapest is that the SPA has slowed the progress of privatization. Before its establishment spontaneous privatization was common but led to the enrichment of managers who were reaping large payoffs for selling the enterprises at bargain prices.

Conclusion

On the optimistic side, the SPA's recent announcement that it will entertain bids for all government enterprises suggests that Hungary may be serious about privatization. Given the possibilities for delay, however, there can be little confidence that privatization in Hungary will succeed or that the SPA has the ability to process and approve a large number of privatizations within a short time.

POLAND

The Polish economy's wrenching reform program has abolished controls on most prices, freed private enterprise, and reduced government subsidies. The result is that inflation has been reduced from nearly 1,000 percent per month in January 1990 to under 2 percent in August 1990. Since then inflation has been edging up. For 1990, Polish inflation was about 250 percent, but that included the explosion in prices in January.[11] Unemployment has been mounting; by the end of December 1990 it had reached more than one million, or 8.3 percent of the work force.[12]

The government budget, however, is in surplus, with the hard currency trade balance the largest ever recorded.[13] The country has a large foreign debt (about $36 billion,[14] or a little over $900 for each individual), while the gross national product per capita is approximately $6,900.[15] Other estimates of per capita income are considerably lower, going down to about $2,000.[16] Estimates of how much of the economy is owned by the government range from 80 percent to 90 percent. About 15 percent of retail shops and restaurants are in private hands as are about 50 percent of all pharmacies.

Notwithstanding the shock treatment and the reductions in subsidies, there have been virtually no bankruptcies, much to the surprise of most observers. Many firms are uneconomic, and the steel mills, most coal mines, and many other large concerns will ultimately have to be closed. Knowing they were going to face hard times, enterprises built up supplies and large bank balances, then refused to pay their suppliers, who in turn withheld payment to *their* suppliers. The banking system may still be making loans to these operations, even though the intention was to eliminate them. One report is that two-thirds of the chemical industry is still receiving government subsidies.

If and when these enterprises go bankrupt, there will be a sharp rise in those out of work, and the unemployment fund will be unable to meet the demand without government help. Privatization will also contribute greatly to unemployment. One-half to two-thirds of the jobs in many big enterprises are redundant. Even in smaller shops and pharmacies, perhaps as many as one-half the workers will be let go under privatization. The agricultural work force needs to be reduced by about two-thirds over the next five years. The generous unemployment allowance (up to 80 percent of a worker's salary) for the first few months of unemployment will put great financial pressure on the government. If the government continues to pay these benefits, it will be forced to print the money, which will escalate inflation. Whether the government has the political will to sustain this high unemployment may determine Poland's future.

Many Poles are skeptical about capitalism and think it is better for all to remain poor than for some to become wealthy while others remain impoverished. Communists painted a picture of capitalism exploiting workers, generating unemployment, and producing wildly fluctuating prices and unstable markets. Lech Walesa, the Solidarity leader, says that Polish society has been demoralized by years of communism and that workers need to learn to work. He has reportedly asserted, however, that the objective is to achieve Western prosperity without having to work hard! Some Poles are concerned that the *nomenklatura* will take over; in numerous cases, former Communist leaders have used this reform period to acquire equipment and small enterprises at rock-bottom prices.

In contrast, public opinion polls show that some 54 percent of the public believe that the government's reform program is "good for the country and in the best national interest." The percentage who support the government has grown in recent months, and two-thirds of the public now agree that the economy should be privatized.[17]

To privatize large enterprises, the government must reassert its ownership of these operations. In the early 1980s, the government set up workers' councils to manage government establishments. As noted above, these councils approve the managing director, set his bonus, which is a significant portion of his income, and can fire him. Those workers' councils are also the main support of Solidarity. The government must transform these worker-run businesses into joint stock corporations before they can be privatized, but in some cases the workers' councils oppose the transformation. Although under the law these workers' councils must approve the changeover, a provision in the law permits the Council of Ministers to order the transformation after consulting with the workers and the managing director, presumably even over their objections. The stringent controls on wages—100 to 500 percent tax on any increase in the wage fund (the total payroll of the operation) over 60 percent of the rate of inflation— bring pressure to bear to permit the conversion. Once privatized, a firm will be largely free to raise wages.

The Parliament has passed a basic privatization law that, among other things, establishes a Ministry for Ownership Transformation. This law also allows for converting enterprises from workers' council management to joint stock corporations and authorizes the sale of 20 percent of the firm's equity to workers at half price, with employees being limited to purchasing no more than the value of their annual salary. (For profitable companies, workers are demanding that they be given a higher percentage of the shares.) The law permits the sale of 30 percent of the corporations through share vouchers issued by the state. Ten percent of the equity can be sold to foreigners. The remaining ownership will be auctioned or otherwise sold, either at the same time or after the vouchers are exercised.

The government fears that many individuals receiving the vouchers will know little about corporate management and that widely diversified ownership may give managers too much leeway. Thus the government has proposed having foreign investment houses establish mutual funds so that the public, using its vouchers, could purchase shares in mutual funds instead of buying stock shares directly.

Although the law does not ban the trade in vouchers, there has been considerable reluctance to permit such a market. Officials fear that voucher trading might discredit the coupon program, but recent news reports indicate that these vouchers may be marketable after all. The program appears similar to the one I proposed for the Soviet Union.

That scheme, described in a newspaper article, would require the government to prepare a schedule listing a limited number of facilities to be privatized each week.[18] The state would also give each individual a voucher for an arbitrary amount, say a thousand units, good only for purchasing shares of stock in government facilities. Individuals would bid for shares, for example, ten units per share for fifty shares of XYZ Company. The firms would then allocate the equity according to the highest bids. If no one bid for a particular enterprise, the government would give the equity to the workers. Individuals could sell their units but only to other nationals, and those that did not want to participate could sell their units to the more entrepreneurial. The ten largest stockholders, together with the three top administrators of the facility, would become the board of directors, with the authority to hire and fire the management and make general policy for the enterprise. This program would speed an equitable process of privatization.

Because privatization takes time, the finance minister has proposed a program of "commercialization" involving the transformation of worker-managed firms into joint stock companies. Although such a conversion is a necessary first step in any privatization program, under commercialization these corporations would remain in government ownership. One-third of the board of directors would be elected by workers' councils; the minister would appoint the rest from names suggested by outside groups, such as chambers of commerce, the Federation of Polish Employers, workers' councils in unrelated industries, and representatives from other industries. The idea is to make these concerns behave a little more like privately owned companies and be more efficient, thus preparing them for privatization. As an inducement to existing workers' councils to give up their authority over these firms, the government proposes to reduce the wage fund tax to allow somewhat higher wages.

The Poles have made less progress than the Hungarians in privatization. The Poles started later (the first reforms date from early 1990) but have moved rapidly in economic reforms since the first of the year. Poland was the first country in Central Europe to legalize private radio and television stations,[19] with several stations already broadcasting. As mentioned above, in September the government announced plans to privatize seven profitable government businesses by December but succeeded in selling equity for only five of the concerns by January. Government officials assert that, by the end of March, one hundred additional large enterprises should be ready for privatization.

The small privatization program, which some claim will move all retailing into private ownership by the end of the year, is to be carried out by local governments. In the main the district and city governments plan to auction the shops. These same authorities will set rents, often using an auction mechanism to arrive at the market rate. About twelve thousand retailing shops (15 percent) had been privatized by July 1990.

Some local governments are imposing limitations on newly privatized stores, so that for a period of time they must continue to offer the same type of merchandise as the government-owned facility. Many fear that food stores will switch to selling high-priced (and high-profit) clothing, so a number of communities propose to offer low rents to shops selling essentials, such as groceries. This attitude reflects little understanding of a market economy.

Since the legalization of private enterprise, numerous open-air stands, selling everything from fruit to video recorders, have sprung up in central areas. Although licenses are required, many, to the distinct unhappiness of the Ministry of Labor, operate without one. Private taxis compete with government-owned taxis; the private taxis appear unregulated, and patrons must bargain with the drivers before the ride.

Reprivatization for Polish citizens will be permitted under laws now being established that will allow former owners and their heirs to claim property but only within a short period. The whole reprivatization time is intended to be short and the claims easily decided. Returning property to previous owners will, nevertheless, slow small privatizations.

Conclusion

Poland faces a difficult task in privatizing its economy. Progress has been slow, and the emphasis on reprivatization is likely to slow it further. The voucher program will be implemented only after considerable delay, if at all. Upcoming sales are likely to generate considerable controversy over whether they were made at too low a price. As more of the economy becomes either private or more efficient, unemployment is likely to rise sharply. The government will have to either reduce unemployment and welfare benefits or give up its struggle to keep the state budget in balance. If the government starts to hand out subsidies or fund expensive social welfare benefits, inflation is likely to be rekindled. (Inflation in December was up sharply, to 5.9 percent over the previous month, and about three times the rate of increase in the July/August period.)[20]

The future of privatization in Poland lies in the actions of the winner of the December presidential election, Lech Walesa. In the election, Walesa criticized Tadeusz Mazowiecki, the prime minister, for privatizing too slowly and yet promising to prevent hardships to workers and to mitigate unemployment.

The strong showing of Stanislaw Tyminski, the unknown Polish-Canadian-Peruvian, in the election raises major problems for reform. Although Tyminski claimed to be a libertarian, that is, an advocate of a totally free market, he put forth no economic program and in fact was highly critical of the government's plans and efforts. Most of his support came from voters expressing dissatisfaction with the economic reform program. Tyminski's defeat of Mazowiecki is viewed as a repudiation of the "shock treatment" approach.

Because Walesa won with an overwhelming mandate, he has strengthened the proreform program by choosing Jan Krzysztof Bielecki as the new prime minister. Bielecki, a young free market advocate, has asserted that he will speed small privatization and that private property and competition are to be the keys to moving the economy forward. Walesa kept Leszek Balcerowicz, the architect of Polish economic reform, as deputy premier and finance minister. These moves indicate that Walesa plans to speed economic reforms and give rise to hopes that Poland may make the transition to a market economy.

CZECHOSLOVAKIA

The Czech government has been outspoken about privatizing its economy but to date has done virtually nothing. President Vaclav Havel apparently prefers a slower approach, while Finance Minister Vaclav Klaus has been pressing for a quick move to a market economy.

Czechoslovakia is the most prosperous of the three countries, with a per capita income of about $9,700.[21] (Other estimates show a much lower income per person, with the lowest being under $4,000.)[22] Its annual inflation rate is only 11 percent, much lower than that of either Hungary or Poland.[23] The country ran a trade surplus of $974 million in 1989, and its foreign debt is reasonably modest and better than that of either Hungary or Poland.

Czechoslovakia, however, is the Central European country with the most pervasive government ownership. Virtually all prices were controlled until January 1, 1991, and most products were subsidized. The government liberalized prices on January 1, 1991, but controls have been retained on basic foods, heating, and transport. Rents were raised some 100 to 200 percent but not freed. The Czech currency was also devalued about 14 percent the same day.

Czechoslovakia is extremely dependent on heavy industry: it produces more than one ton of steel per capita, and about 70 percent of its exports involve machinery and heavy engineering. Two-fifths of its exports have been going to the Soviet Union, which may not buy them in the future. Moreover, East Germany, Czechoslovakia's second-biggest CMEA partner, has just canceled big contracts.

The Czechs recognize that they have been living on their capital and that they cannot continue to do so. At the end of the Second World War they were the richest country in Europe, having escaped the bombing during the war while the Germans invested heavily in Czechoslovakian factories. Being relatively prosperous, however, the Czechs feel less urgency about making the shift to a market economy and are less willing to give up the security of the Communist system. The public generally mistrusts privatization, fearing unemployment and higher prices. Many cannot accept that there is no third way.

In April the government passed legislation allowing private enterprise. Some 300,000 entrepreneurs have registered. Because many have been unable to find operating space in buildings still owned by the government, however, many if not most of these enterprises have yet to open.

The Finance Ministry intends to sell off some 70 percent of large enterprises within five years. As of the middle of January 1991, legislation to privatize larger enterprises had not yet passed Parliament and appeared mired in political dispute. The finance minister, Vaclav Klaus, plans to market firms to foreign investors, sell them to workers through employee stock option plans, or auction the companies through a voucher program. For the first two years, the state will retain a large share of the stock.

The Finance Ministry's vouchers, which would be offered cheaply to the public but which could not be resold, would permit citizens to purchase shares in enterprises. Citizens could buy additional vouchers at higher prices; foreign buyers could acquire these vouchers at greater cost. These vouchers would carry a nominal value and be used to purchase directly up to 20 percent of a firm's equity; another 10 percent could be purchased through mutual funds. After the sale of stock for vouchers, some stock would be sold to citizens for Czech crowns; finally foreigners would be able to purchase stocks. There has been no decision on whether foreigners would be able to buy land.

The Czechoslovakian Parliament approved a law, effective December 1, 1990, to auction about 100,000 small shops and enterprises that were nationalized during forty years of communism. The exact extent of the privatization has yet to be settled. To prevent black marketers from using their profits to purchase these assets, buyers must show their 1990 income tax returns. Bidders must purchase a shop's current inventory, and food stores will be required to continue to sell basic food items for at least one year. Apparently the law makes no provision to benefit existing shop personnel, although the original plan gave preference to those who had worked in the enterprises before the 1989 revolution.

Earlier the Czechoslovakian Parliament had approved a program to return to the original owner or his or her heirs the small businesses, factories, shops, and other property confiscated under Communist rule. All property nationalized from 1955 to 1959 is to be returned in its present condition: If it has been allowed to deteriorate, that is how it will be returned; if it has been improved, the previous owners will receive the improvements. If changes are so significant as to make return unrealistic, the law allows for monetary compensation.

Conclusion

Czechoslovakia has made little progress in privatization. Although small privatization appears to be going forward, reprivatization will keep the sale of all small businesses from being completed this year. A substantial portion of retailing, restaurants, small services, housing, commercial buildings, and other small businesses, however, should be privatized by the end of 1991.

Large-scale privatization of major business will take substantially longer. Legislation has not yet been introduced, and valuation will be a major problem. The voucher scheme as currently planned is complicated and may easily fail. Opposition by employees may slow progress.

The success of privatization will depend on the outcome of the political struggle between Vaclav Klaus, the finance minister, and Vaclav Havel, the president. Havel wants to go slowly to keep unemployment from rising sharply. Klaus, in contrast, wants to move ahead quickly. Klaus seems to be gaining power, having recently been elected the head of the Civic Forum over the president's choice.

In addition, the struggle of the Slovaks to gain greater autonomy may seriously compromise any program for economic change. At the moment all major legislation must be approved by the governments of the Czech republic and the Slovak republic as well as the central government. Many Slovaks, however, are demanding complete control over their own economy.

OVERALL CONCLUSIONS

The difficulties in privatizing the economies of Central Europe are colossal. Unless a massive, determined, and accelerated program is launched to shift the tools of production into private hands, economic reforms will fail. The depressing election results in Poland indicate to politicians from Prague to Moscow that an aggressive movement toward a market economy is likely to bring political defeat. Without privatization these countries will remain inefficient, producing poor-quality goods and poor people.

The greatest peril that these nations face is falling prey to the Argentine model of a declining economy and periods of democracy followed by periods of military rule. If this results, Western Europe will face a growing crisis of illegal immigration from Central Europe as the enterprising, the young, and the well educated attempt to migrate to the more prosperous West. This presents a dilemma both for the West—many in the European Community fear that an influx of illegal immigrants will steal good jobs (in truth, these people would contribute strongly to growth)—and for those Central European countries that will experience a major brain drain. Thus, the outcome will be continued instability in Central Europe, the failure of democracy, and a movement toward dictatorial solutions.

NOTES

1. Irwin L. Collier, Jr., and Horst Siebert, "The Economic Integration of Post-Wall Germany," paper given at the American Economic Association meetings in Washington, D.C., December 1990.
2. "First Sale of State Holdings a Disappointment in Poland," *New York Times*, January 14, 1991, p. C1.
3. *Statistical Abstract of the United States*, 1990, table 1483, p. 860, and table 1438, p. 832.
4. *Statistical Abstract of the United States*, 1990, table 1446, p. 840.
5. "Survey Perestroika," *The Economist*, April 28, 1990, p. 6.
6. "East Europe Offers Investors Big Profits and Big Perils," *Wall Street Journal*, January 11, 1991, p. A8 (data from PlanEcon, a consulting group in Washington, D.C.).
7. "Hungary Acts to Privatize," *New York Times*, January 11, 1991, p. C8.
8. "Hungary Puts All State Industry up for Sale," *Financial Times*, October 19, 1990, p. 3.
9. "Hungary Acts to Privatize," *New York Times*.
10. "Hungary Rift on Asset Sale," *New York Times*, November 8, 1990, p. C7.
11. "Poland Had Record Trade Surplus in 1990, But . . . ," Reuters, January 9, 1991.
12. "Unemployment Rise Slows in Poland," *Financial Times*, January 8, 1991, p. 3.
13. Ibid.
14. *Statistical Abstract of the United States*, 1990, table 1483, p. 860.
15. *Statistical Abstract of the United States*, 1990, table 1446, p. 840.
16. "Survey Perestroika," p. 6.
17. "First Steps to Privatization," *Gazeta International*, December 6, 1990, p. 6.
18. Thomas Gale Moore, "A Privatization Program for Gorbachev," *Wall Street Journal*, May 30, 1990.
19. Polska Agencja Prasowa News Agency, October 26, 1990.
20. Donosy (an electronic news service operating out of Poland), no. 427, January 15, 1991.
21. *Statistical Abstract of the United States*, 1990, table 1446, p. 840.
22. "Survey Perestroika," p. 6.
23. "East Europe Offers Investors Big Profits," *Wall Street Journal*.
24. *Financial Times*, January 4, 1991, p. 2.